PERFECT PETS

page 2

page 14

**Story illustrated by
Martin Chatterton**

Heinemann

Before Reading

In this story

Silly Sid

Tricky words

- wanted
- goldfish
- cage
- parrot

Introduce these tricky words and help the reader when they come across them later!

Story starter

Silly Sid is a bit silly. One day, he decided that he wanted a pet but he wasn't sure what sort of pet to have.

Silly Sid Wants a Pet

Silly Sid wanted a pet.

"I want a goldfish," said Silly Sid.

"I will put my goldfish in this cage."

Silly Sid went to the pet shop.

"I am silly," said Silly Sid.
"I can't put a goldfish in this!"

"I want a parrot," said Silly Sid.

"I will put my parrot in this cage."

Is Silly Sid being silly?

Silly Sid went to the pet shop.

"I am silly," said Silly Sid.
"I can't put a parrot in this!"

"I am not so silly,"
said Silly Sid. "I will
put my parrot in this!"

Quiz

Text Detective

- Why couldn't Silly Sid put a parrot in his cage?
- Do you have a pet, or would you like to have a pet?

Word Detective

- **Phonic Focus:** Final phonemes

  Page 4: Find a word ending with the phoneme 'sh'.
- Page 10: Find a little word inside the word 'went'.
- Page 11: Find a word that means the opposite of 'can'.

Super Speller

Read these words:

put   will

Now try to spell them!

HA! HA! HA!

Q What do you get if you cross a centipede with a parrot?

A A walkie-talkie.

Find out about

- What pets need

Tricky words

- what
- does
- water
- drink
- doesn't
- someone

Introduce these tricky words and help the reader when they come across them later!

Text starter

There are some things that all pets need to be happy and healthy. All pets need food and most pets need water and a bed to sleep on. But the one thing all pets need is someone to love them.

Pet Care

What do pets need?

All pets need food to eat.

What food does this pet eat?

Hamsters like to eat seeds and nuts.

What do pets need?

Most pets need water to drink.

Does this pet drink water?

No, it doesn't ...

... but this pet does!

What do pets need?

Most pets need a bed to sleep on.

Does this pet need a bed?

No, it doesn't ...

... but this pet does!

What do pets need?

All pets need someone
to love them.

Does someone love this pet?

YES!

Quiz

Text Detective

- Which pet does not need a bed?
- What do all pets need? Why?

Word Detective

- **Phonic Focus:** Final phonemes
  Page 16: Find a word ending with the phoneme 'll'.
- Page 19: Find the word 'pet' twice on the page.
- Page 20: Find a word that means 'rest'.

Super Speller

Read these words:

eat   bed

Now try to spell them!

HA! HA! HA!

Q What do you call a donkey with three legs?

A A wonkey.